HAPPY HENS

Story and Pictures by
SHARON KRAUS

Copyright © 2024 Sharon Kraus.

All rights reserved. No part of this book may be reproduced, stored, or transmitted by any means—whether auditory, graphic, mechanical, or electronic—without written permission of both publisher and author, except in the case of brief excerpts used in critical articles and reviews. Unauthorized reproduction of any part of this work is illegal and is punishable by law.

ISBN: 979-8-89419-161-4 (sc)
ISBN: 979-8-89419-162-1 (hc)
ISBN: 979-8-89419-163-8 (e)

Because of the dynamic nature of the Internet, any web addresses or links contained in this book may have changed since publication and may no longer be valid. The views expressed in this work are solely those of the author and do not necessarily reflect the views of the publisher, and the publisher hereby disclaims any responsibility for them.

One Galleria Blvd., Suite 1900, Metairie, LA 70001
(504) 702-6708

About the Story

In this story the author shares facts about chickens and photo of different breeds.

There are pictures of chickens with other animals and pictures of baby chicks. There are chickens inside a chicken coop and outside enjoying the sunshine.

The story has interesting information about chickens and talks about the entertaining things chickens do.

This is a story about Happy Hens. You will see Scarlett, Sapphire, Sofia, Saffron, Sage, Selena, Stella and Serenity, as they go about their days. You will see why they are happy hens.

Hens are happy when they get to go outside. They like to wander around looking for seeds and bugs in the grass. They scratch around to find things to eat. Happy hen chatter to each other while they enjoy the nice days.

They clean up whatever grain the horses drop on the ground. Sweet feed is a treat for the chickens.

Sometimes they seem to think the horses water is better than theirs. The horses don't mind sharing with the chickens.

Hens are happy when they get treats like watermelon, squash and pumpkins. They eat the seeds and everything till there's nothing left but paper thin skin. They like berries, fruits and vegetables of almost any kind.

Happy hens love going in the garden and scratching around in the dirt for worms and bugs. They are great bug control for the garden. Herbs like garlic, oregano, thyme, calendula and other plants and flowers that are grown in the garden, are fed to the chickens for more flavor in their food and to keep them healthy.

A hen usually lays an egg about every other day. The eggs will only grow into chicks if the hen has mated with a rooster. The rooster fertilizes the hens eggs. If there is no rooster, hens still lay eggs. They are used for eating instead of hatching.

A group of eggs is called a clutch. A hen sits on eggs in the nest to keep them warm. She will sit on them until they hatch.

A hen that likes to sit on eggs is called a broody hen. A hen that is broody will sit on eggs and want to stay in the nesting box even without leaving to eat so she can stay with the eggs.

Hens sit on their eggs to hatch them. They stay on their nesting box where the eggs are safe and protected. The hens cover the eggs with their wings to keep them warm.

They love their chicks and are very good Mothers.

Eggs can also be taken after the hens lay them. They can be put in an incubator to be hatched. Chicks can also be purchased at farm stores. They sell many different breeds.

Everyone loves chicks! They are so cute and fluffy.

A favorite breed, because of their curly plumage, is the 'Frizzle' chicken. Their ornamental feathers make them good to show at chicken shows.

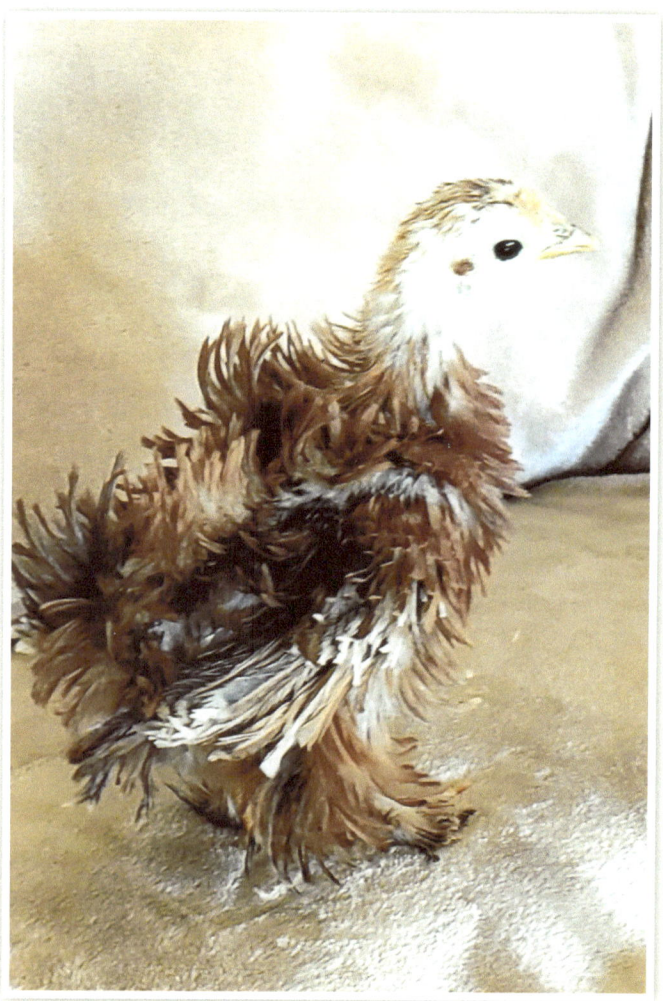

Silkies are another favorite for showing because of their silky, furlike feathers. Their gentle nature makes them good pets.

Mother hens cluck to talk to their chicks. A deep duck means 'follow me'. A high pitched cluck means 'food'. Chicks always know their Mother's clucks. Hens bok-bok to each other and chicks peep-peep.

Chicks grow fast. When females are less than a year old, they are called pullets. When they are older than a year they are hens. Baby chickens are chicks. Young male chickens are cockerels and grown males are roosters.

As chicks grow, they start developing red combs and wattles. The males will be larger and more brightly colored than females. Soon after combs and wattles develop, cockerels will begin to crow a good cock-a-doodle do. The French say a crow says 'coquerico'. In Spanish its 'Quiquiriqui' and in German roosters say 'kikeriki'.

A young chicken starting to grow a comb.

A rooster with a full comb and wattles, stretched up and crowing.

When chickens are grown they get other distinctive features too. Their feathers change to colors they will stay. Different breeds have different colored feathers. These beautiful Polish crested chickens are well liked because of their unusual looks, with feathers covering their head, and their calm nature.

Another breed of chickens,
are Buff Orpingtons, who are hardy and friendly.

Bantams are smaller sized chickens. There are many different colored Bantams. This one is a booted bantam because of the feathers on his feet.

Araucana's are different colors and lay colorful eggs.
Sometimes called 'Easter egg' chickens, they lay blue and light green eggs.

Golden Laced Wyandotte's are gentle and good egg layers

Leghorns are a very popular breed of chicken as they are good layers

Leghorns have big red combs on top of their heads that keep them cool.

Roosters protect the hens and chicks. They are bigger than hens and have very pretty feathers and long tail feathers.

They do a chicken dance when they find a hen they like. A rooster will bring a hen food and calls out to all the hens, then does a dance, circling around her. If she likes him she will stay and if she doesn't she will walk away.

Happy hens make friends with other animals on the farm.

They make friends with each other and even make friends with other birds and squirrels that come around to eat some cracked corn.

They especially like the people that take care of them. Chickens can make good pets. You can show them in 4-H shows. You can save feathers to do craft project with. And there are a lot of things to make and do with eggs and shells.

Happy hens like to scoop out nests in the dirt. They like to lay in them and roll around and take dust baths. They also keep themselves clean by preening their feathers. To preen, they run their beak through their feathers.

Happy hens love rhustling through fallen leaves. They look under the leaves for bugs. They are curious and like to see what's going on around the farm.

They feel cozy and safe in their chicken coop. They have perches and ladders to sit on. When it gets dark outside, they all go inside where they are safe from predators. There are small doors to go in and out of, that are closed at night.

They have roosts that are up off the ground that they like to sleep on. The nesting boxes and the entire coop are covered in shavings that give them soft places to lay. Plants like lavender, chamomile and jasmine make the coop smell good and keep the hens happy.

Keeping hens happy is easy when they have a nice place to live.

Vocabulary

Broody - a hen that likes sitting on eggs. She has decided she wants to be a mother.

Clutch - a group of eggs that are incubated together, to hatch at the same time.

Comb - the fleshy protrusion on the top of a chickens head.

Crest - the billowy feather hat on top of certain breeds, such as silkies and polish.

Layers - hens that lay eggs.

Plumage - a birds feathers

Preening - is a chickens way of grooming. It keeps feathers clean and reapplies oils to their feathers. Sometimes they preen each other.

Roost - a branch, board or bar where chickens perch at night.

Wattles - the fleshy jowls at the base of a chickens beak.

References

Beautiful Chickens
by Christie Aschwanden

A Guide to Raising Chickens
by Gail Damerow

Breed Associations can offer more information on different breeds of chickens.

Other things to do with chickens include the following. Googleing any of these will provide more information.

Showing at 4-H or chicken shows

Do crafts with feathers such as fishing flies.

Grow seeds in egg shells cracked in half.

Make an Easter egg tree.

Ukranian Easter Eggs

Egg dyeing, try using natural dyes.

About the Author

The author is the mother of six children. She and her kids raised horses, cows, sheep, goats and chickens in a small midwestern town. This made for an interesting and entertaining life.

Forty years later, she is still keeping chickens and sharing eggs with others.